WordPress for Beginners

The Easy Step-by-Step Guide to Creating

A Website with WordPress

By Christine John

WordPress for Beginners

The Easy Step-by-Step Guide to Creating

A Website with WordPress

Website: www.christinejohnbooks.com

Email: christinejohnbooks@gmail.com

Disclaimer:

Although the author has made every effort to ensure that the information in this book was correct at press time, the author does not assume and hereby disclaims any liability to any party for any loss, damage, or disruption caused by errors or omissions, whether such errors or omissions result from negligence, accident, or any other cause.

Table of Contents

Introduction 5

   What is WordPress? 5

   The Benefits of Using WordPress 6

   What You Need to Use WordPress..7

Register a Domain Name...9

   How to Register a Domain Name...12

Set Up Web Hosting 20

How to Set Up Web Hosting..21

   How to Set Your Domain Name DNS 23

Entering Your Website 27

Inside Your WordPress Website 32

   How to Change Your Password and Log Out...............................35

Management Features on the Left Sidebar 37

   How to Change the Appearance of Your Website........................37

   How to Change the Theme..37

How to Change the Settings of Your Site 40

   General Settings..40

   Reading Settings..41

How to Create a Post..43

How to Create a Page..45

   Delete a Page 47

How to Upload Media 49

   Delete Media...53

How to Install Plugins 55

   Install and Activate a Plugin...55

   Delete a Plugin 58

Other Useful Tools for Your WordPress Site 60

How to Manage Comments 66

    Remove Comments from Pages 66

    Remove Comments from Posts 68

    Delete a Widget 77

    Remove a Widget.. 78

Optimize Your WordPress Site for the Search Engines 80

    Change Permalinks... 80

    Optimize the Titles of Your Posts for SEO 82

    Optimize the Descriptions of Your Posts/Pages 82

    Optimize Your Images 83

    Optimize Your Tags 83

Conclusion 85

About the Author 86

Other Books Written by Christine John 87

Introduction

*I am pleased to present to you the updated version of this book **WordPress for Beginners: The Easy Step-by-Step Guide to Creating a Website with WordPress**. The internet is always changing and there are some websites that may be out of date or that may no longer exist, so I may have changed or removed some of the links from this book. Also there are a couple of plugins that were listed in this book that are out of date so I have removed them and included more up to date plugins that you can use to increase functionality of your website.*

I discovered WordPress a few years ago by accident. I was looking for an easier way to design a website without having any technical knowledge. I came across WordPress on the search engine results page. Since then I have been using this blogging software to design websites for myself, my family, and my friends. I even made a little side business designing websites for other people.

There is no better time to design a website than right now. WordPress has made it so easy to build your own website without having to learn any HTML codes or being forced to pay thousands of dollars on a professional web designer. You can set up a website in less than an hour with this amazing software. But WordPress is so much more than just a blogging platform.

What is WordPress?

WordPress started as a blogging system in 2003, but has been developed since then into an open source content management system which you can use for just about anything you can imagine. You are not limited to just a blog. You can build a full blown website with this software. You can build an e-commerce store, create a portfolio of your art, or make a photo journal.

Teachers, professionals, large corporations, authors, students, and private individuals all use WordPress as a blogging platform to get their message across to their readers on the World Wide Web. It is almost as easy as using a Word processor.

WordPress offers two versions of its popular software that you can use. You can either use the free hosted version of Wordpress.com or the self-hosted version offered at Wordpress.org. But this book will be focussing mainly on the self-hosted version of WordPress.

The Benefits of Using WordPress

WordPress has made it easy for the average person to create a website for personal use or business. You don't have to worry about learning any complicated HTML codes or CSS in order to build a professional-looking website. It doesn't matter how complex your site may become, WordPress makes it easy for you to edit and manage the content on your site. There are many other benefits of using WordPress.

WordPress allows you to increase the functionality of your website with the use of special tools called Plugins. All you need to do is install a plugin and activate it for it be functional.

WordPress provides a user-friendly interface. You don't have to worry about contacting a web developer to make changes to your website. This software makes it easy for you to update your site's content.

You can change the appearance of your website in seconds using professional-looking WordPress themes. There are hundreds of themes that you can choose from on the Wordpress.org website. As mentioned before, you don't need to know HTML or CSS to change the theme.

By using the WordPress software your site will be indexed quickly by Google. This search engine loves WordPress and you can easily optimize your site by installing some very powerful SEO plugins.

One of the interesting features of WordPress is its built-in comments function. You can use Comments to build rapport with your readers, provide customer service or to simply interact with them. It is a great tool that you can use to get feedback on the content of your site. The comments you receive on your site are a great way to learn more about what your readers are looking for and how you can improve the functionality of your site.

What You Need to Use WordPress

Installing the WordPress software is very easy and there is not much that you need. The basic things you need are a computer with internet connection, a domain name and a web hosting account. In the chapters that follow I will show you how to choose the right domain name and how to register it and set up web hosting.

If you are interested in building your own website, then you have picked up the right book. This comprehensive guide will show you everything you need to know to set up your own website. This book covers all the important topics such as:

1. Registering a domain name

2. Setting up web hosting

3. Choosing a theme for your site

4. Creating pages and posts

5. Installing and activating plugins

6. Managing and editing your site's content

7. Optimizing your site for the search engines

Assuming that you are computer literate, and that you are familiar with the internet and email, you should not have any problems using this guide to design your own WordPress website. This book will guide you step-by-step and you will see how easy it is to create your own site in minutes.

Register a Domain Name

Before you can create a website you need to first come up with a proper domain name and then register it at a domain name registering company. Here are a few tips for coming up with a great domain name.

Try to come up with words related to your niche market or the type of website you want to create. Write down as many words as you can.

You can use a dictionary and a thesaurus to find as many words as you can come up with for your domain name, or you can use Google's Keyword Planner. Go to https://adwords.google.com/KeywordPlanner. If you do not have one, you will need to first sign up for a Google email (Gmail) account.

If you need to get keyword ideas then you will have to sign into your Google Adwords account using your Gmail address to get started. Once you are signed in, click on "**Search for new keywords and ad group ideas**". Type a name in the search box under Your Product or Service and click on the blue button **Get Ideas**.

In the search results you will see how many people have searched for information pertaining to that particular keyword.

The following image is a bar chart showing the average number of searches per month and just below the chart you can see the actual number of monthly searches for the keyword you chose.

If more than a thousand people have searched for your chosen keyword in the past 12 months then you have a very popular keyword. Based on the results you can use that keyword as your domain name.

Once you are satisfied with your domain name, you can then register it at your chosen domain name registration company. There are many domain registration companies online, but the one I use is www.domainorb.com. You pay less than $10 per year for your domain name.

There are other sites where you can register a domain name such as:

www.godaddy.com

www.names.co.uk

www.123-reg.co.uk

www.crazydomains.co.uk

www.websitepalace.com

www.namecheap.com

How to Register a Domain Name

1. To register your domain name go to http://www.domainorb.com.

2. Enter your domain name in the form provided and click **Check it!**

3. If the domain name you have chosen is unavailable, then click **Search Again**.

4. Enter another domain name, ensure that .com is selected, and click **Submit**.

New Domain Registration

5. When you find a domain name that is available, click **Update Selections/Continue**.

6. Click on **Checkout** and then you will be taken to a page where you can create an account with Domainorb.com.

Current Cart Contents ?

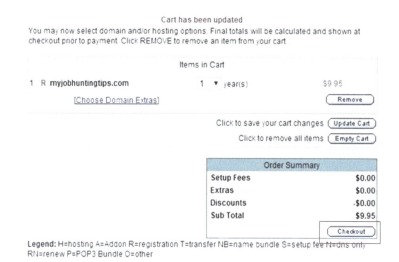

Cart has been updated
You may now select domain and/or hosting options. Final totals will be calculated and shown at checkout prior to payment. Click REMOVE to remove an item from your cart.

	Items in Cart		
1 R myjobhuntingtips.com	1 ▾ year(s)		$9.95
[Choose Domain Extras]			Remove

Click to save your cart changes Update Cart
Click to remove all items Empty Cart

Order Summary	
Setup Fees	$0.00
Extras	$0.00
Discounts	-$0.00
Sub Total	$9.95
	Checkout

Legend: H=hosting A=Addon R=registration T=transfer NB=name bundle S=setup fee N=dns only RN=renew P=POP3 Bundle O=other

7. On the **Create an Account** page, assuming that you don't have an account at Domainorb.com, choose your Username and Password and enter your contact information. If you don't have a business then you can skip the part about organisation name and job title. You can also leave the last section about Nameservers blank. You will enter this information later after you purchase web hosting.

8. Ensure that you have filled in the form completely and correctly and then click on **Submit** at the bottom. You will be taken to the invoice page that shows the number of domain names you are registering and how much it will cost.

9. On the Invoice page, read through the information and ensure that it is correct. Once you are satisfied, scroll to the bottom and choose your payment options. Don't forget to click the check box next to the **Terms of Service** and then click on **Submit**.

INVOICE
DomainOrb.com
13428 Maxella Avenue
Marina Del Rey, CA 90292
whs-helpdesk@domainorb.com

Order Info   Order Date: 05-05-2014
Name: Total Domain: $9.95
Company:
Phone: Sub Total: $9.95
Email Address   Tax Due: $0.00
                               Total Due: $9.95

Your purchase overview

Type/Qty Description   Amount
R   myjobhuntingtips.com   Domain for 1 year(s) $9.95

Domain profile choices
(Required for domain orders)

10. You will be taken to another page that says that your credit card will be charged. Click on the **Continue to Payment** button.

Your credit card will be charged $9.95

Please note: After completing your payment the process may take some time, depending upon Internet traffic.
Please be patient and wait it out!
Thank You!

Continue to Payment

2CO is an authorized retailer for goods and services provided by DomainOrb.com.

Click here to cancel

11. This next page is a secure page where you can choose the currency that you want to pay in. This page is powered by 2Checkout.com and you should see the heading Corridor Services. Once you have selected the currency you want to pay in for your domain name registration, click the green button that says **Continue to Billing Information**.

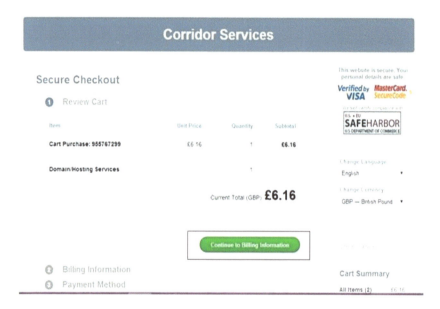

12. On the Secure Checkout page, enter your contact details and then click the green button **Continue to Payment Method**.

13. Once again on the Secure Checkout page, choose your payment method. You can either pay by your debit/credit card or by PayPal. If you decide to use a debit/credit card, enter your card details in the form fields provided. Make sure that you click the checkbox next to Terms of Service and then click **Submit**.

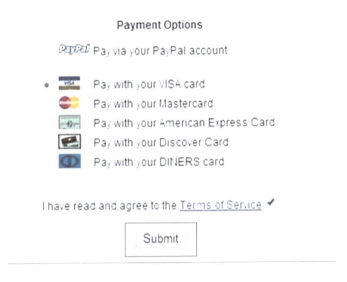

14. On the next page you will see that your payment has been processed. Click the orange button **Finalize Your Order**.

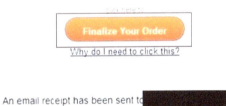

On the final page you will see that your payment process is complete.

Payment Process Complete

Thank You!

Total Payment Amount: $9.95
Transaction ID: 205270301980
Payment Description: -Domain

Your order will be processed automatically upon receiving notification of payment.

*If you paid via echeck, your order will be processed upon the echeck clearing.
(This usually takes up to 4 days.)

If you have any questions regarding your payment, please contact our support department.

Thank you!
DomainOrb.com

Registration of your domain name is complete.

You should receive an email of the invoice of your purchase of your domain name and the amount it cost. The email shows your order summary and billing information.

There are two important points that you must keep in mind when you register a domain name:

You may not transfer a domain name for 60 days after its purchase or for 60 days after you change any registrant contact information. This rule was set by the Internet Corporation for Assigned Names and Numbers (ICANN) and this is a standard rule for all domain name registrars.

For example, if you registered a domain name at Domainorb.com and wanted to transfer the domain name to a web host such as Bluehost.com, then you would have to wait 60 days before you can transfer your domain name. Also if you changed your address after you registered your domain name then you cannot transfer the domain name for 60 days.

You should not register your domain name with the same company you are going to purchase web hosting from. The reason is that you may face problems in the future when you decide that you no longer want to use that company's web hosting services and want to transfer your domain name to a different web host.

For example, if you registered your domain name at Webhost1.com and also purchased web hosting services from that site, and you wanted to transfer your domain name to Webhost2.com, then webhost1.com might give you problems and may not want to let you transfer your domain name so easily.

You might be charged a lot of money to transfer your domain name or go through a lot of trouble to unlock it so that you can transfer it. Therefore, always keep your domain name with your domain registrar. That way you always have control of your domain name and you can assign it to another web host if you are dissatisfied with the one you're with.

Set Up Web Hosting

A web host is a type of internet hosting service which stores your website and then transmits it on the internet for people to view. There are thousands of companies on the internet offering web hosting services.

For a new online entrepreneur trying to start an internet business, finding a good web host can be a little overwhelming. It may be tempting to purchase cheap hosting services from a web host, but you should not select a web host based on price alone. There are other factors you should consider before choosing a company to host your website or blog.

The web host you choose should be reliable and provide support immediately. If you have a problem with your website, you want a web host that will respond quickly to your query. Look for a web host that provides 24/7 support.

Ensure that your web host has PHP version 5.2.4 or greater and MySQL version 5.0 or greater. PHP is a scripting language that is suitable for web development. MySQL is a database management system which you can use to add, access and process data stored in a computer database. A database is a structured collection of data such as a shopping list, a picture gallery or information from a corporate network.

I recommend the following web hosts to host your domain:

http://www.JustHost.com

http://www.BlueHost.com

http://www.Hostgator.com

How to Set Up Web Hosting

I use Justhost.com to host my domain so I will show you how to set up your domain with the same web host.

1. Go to http://www.justhost.com and click **Sign Up Now**.

2. Next choose your hosting plan. Although the starter plan is the cheapest, I recommend that you select the Plus plan because in the future if you decide to create more websites under the Plus plan Just Host allows you to add unlimited websites.

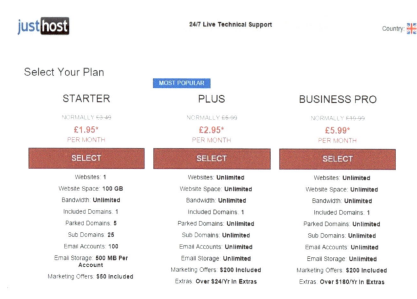

3. Since you already registered a domain name, under the section 'I Have a Domain Name' type in your domain name and then click **Next**.

4. On the next page under Account Information enter your contact details, i.e. your name, address, phone number and email. Under Package Information, select your Account Plan. Then under Billing Information enter your credit card details and select Personal next to Purpose of the Account.

5. Ensure that the check box next to the Confirmation statement is selected. This ensures that you have read and agree to the terms and conditions of use. Then click **Next**.

6. Follow the instructions to complete your web hosting account set up. An email will be sent to you to confirm that your web hosting has been set up. The web host will also include the Nameservers to use to link your domain name to your web host.

How to Set Your Domain Name DNS

DNS stands for Domain Name Server. It is also referred to as simply Nameserver for short. Once you have set up hosting services your web host would have emailed you the DNS information.

Once you have the information just go to the site where you registered your domain name and update the nameserver records. Your domain registrar will provide instructions on how to do this. Enter the DNS information that your web host gave you. It looks like this:

NS1.hostname.com

NS2.hostname.com

It may take up to 48 hours for the nameservers to take effect and to propagate the internet, but when it is done your domain name will be linked to your web host. Also when you type your domain name in the address bar of your web browser you will be able to see your website live on the web.

For example, let's say you registered the domain name Myjobhuntingtips.com at Domainorb.com. Now you want to link your domain name to the web host, which is Justhost.com. If you used Domainorb.com to register your domain name, then follow these instructions:

1. Go to http://www.domainorb.com and click **Member Login**.

2. Enter your username and password and click **Submit**.

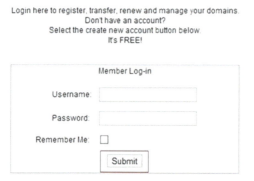

3. Click **View/Edit** next to "Number of domains in your account".

Account Information

Number of domains in your account	4	View/Edit
Domains expiring within 30 Days	0	View/Edit
Domains currently expired	0	View/Edit
Domain transfer requests in progress	0	View/Edit
Domains listed for sale	0	View/Edit
Other items in your account	0	View/Edit

4. Click the letter **'M'**, which stands for 'Manage' in the same row as the domain name you want to change.

Total Records: 4 GLOBAL **Auto Renew** Toggle: [All ON] [All OFF]

[Domain Name] [Expires]

	10-07-2014	M R S
myjobhuntingtips.com	05-05-2015 AR	M R S
	07-15-2014	M R S
	06-13-2014	M R S

<< 1 >>

Icon Legend:
M = Manage   R = Renew   S = Sell
FS = For Sale   H = Has Hosting   AR = Auto Renew

5. Click **Change Nameservers**.

Protect Your Domain Privacy

ID PROTECT

Shield Yourself From Spam, Identity Theft, Data Mining & Name Hijackers

Contact Information

Email Forwarding

Edit DNS Records

Change Nameservers

Nameserver Registration

Expiration Date: 11-15-2013
Nameservers: Custom

>> FAQ Page <<
>> Definitions Page <<

Domain locking

✔ Domain locking

Save

(Note: Some tld's do not support domain locking.)

Auto Renewal

6. Next to the word 'Use' click the arrow and select **Custom Nameservers** from the drop down menu.

7. In the first text box enter **ns1.justhost.com**. In the second text box enter **ns2.justhost.com**.

8. Then click **Submit**. The page will then say 'Dns modification success'.

Assign Nameservers

Dns modification success

9. Click **Logout** and you're done.

You just have to wait about 48 to 72 hours for your domain name to be linked to your web host and become active on the internet.

Entering Your Website

At this stage you should have registered your domain name, created a web hosting account, and set your domain name DNS to point to your web host.

To check that your domain name is linked to your web host simply type the domain name in the address bar and press the Enter key on your keyboard.

As an example, I have registered the domain name Myjobhuntingtips.com with Domainorb.com. I signed up for web hosting at Justhost.com. I have already changed the nameservers so that my domain is linked to my web host.

You can see from the image above that the domain name MyJobHuntingTips.com is linked to Justhost.com.

Now you can move on to the next step which is setting up your WordPress website.

To set up WordPress you need to go through your web host. In this case I am using Justhost.com as my web host.

1. Log in to Justhost.com. Ensure that the Hosting tab has been selected.

2. Click on the WordPress icon on the cPanel located under the Website section.

3. Click **Install** to install the WordPress software.

4. Click the arrow to select the domain name where you want the WordPress software to be installed to. Then click **Check Domain**.

5. Two check boxes will appear. First click the check box **Show Advanced Options**.

6. A drop down list will appear. Enter the title of your website and change your admin username and password to whatever you want it to be. Please ensure that you do not use the word 'admin' as your username because it makes it very easy for hackers to hack into your website.

7. Make sure that the check box where it says '**Automatically create a new database for this installation**' is selected.

8. Click on the check box next to the statement '**I have read the terms and conditions of the GPLv2**' and the click **Install Now**.

Depending on how fast your browser is, the installation of the WordPress software should take less than a minute. When the installation is complete click on **View Credentials** at the top of the page.

You will see a notification that shows you how to access your new WordPress website. It shows your Site and Login URLs, your admin username and password to access the site.

An email will also be sent to you containing instructions on how to access your new WordPress website.

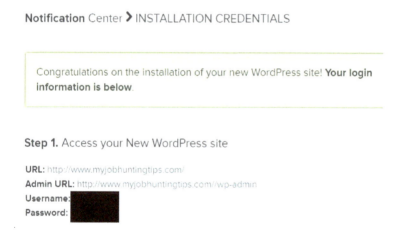

Once the installation is complete you can close the window and log out of your web host account.

To login to WordPress, simply type in your address bar:

http://www.yoursite.com/wp-admin (Replace 'yoursite' with your domain name)

Enter your login details such as your username and password in the WordPress dialog box as shown below:

Username

Password

Remember Me   Log In

Inside Your WordPress Website

In order to make changes to your website, you need to get to the admin section of your site, which is known as the Dashboard where you can use all the different functions to edit the appearance of your website, create new pages and posts and much more.

The Dashboard is the control panel where you can manage your comments, publish your content, and many other things. The dashboard operates behind the scenes of your site. It is referred to as the "backend" of your site that only you can see.

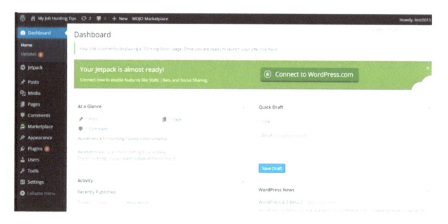

The "frontend" is what the outside world can see when they visit your site. Because you just installed WordPress your website will look very plain as no changes have been made to your site yet. However, you will be using the tools on your dashboard to change the appearance of your site and to publish content.

If you were to go to your website now as a visitor, you would not be able to see the frontend yet because it will display a message that "I just installed WordPress free at Mojo Marketplace..." This message will disappear once you have completed the setup of your website and launched the site for the world to see. You will learn how to do this in a later chapter.

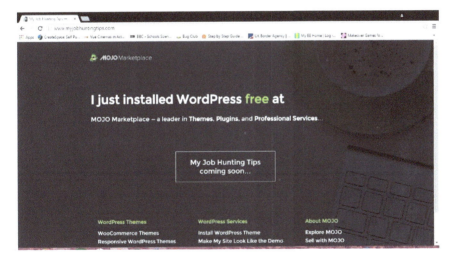

How to Switch Between the Front End and Back End of Your Website

For the purpose of giving you instructions on how to make changes to your website, I will be using the domain www.myjobhuntingtips.com as an example of how to navigate your site.

1. Log in to your website. When you login you will find that you are at the backend of your website which is the Dashboard.

2. Hover the cursor (your mouse) over 'My Job Hunting Tips' at the top left corner in the black area of your screen.

3. Click either **My Job Hunting Tips** or **Visit Site**. This will take you to the frontend of the website.

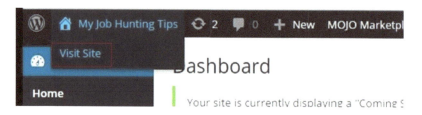

4. To return to the backend of the website, i.e. the Dashboard, hover the cursor over **My Job Hunting Tips** in the top left black area of your screen.

5. Click **Dashboard**. This will take you back to the admin panel of the website.

Now we will go through each feature of the dashboard and I will give you step-by-step instructions on how to make changes to your site.

How to Change Your Password and Log Out

1. On the Dashboard, move the cursor (your mouse) to the upper right corner of your screen and let the cursor hover over the word **Howdy**.

2. Click **Edit My Profile**.

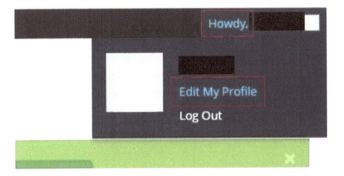

3. To change your password, scroll down to the bottom of the screen and enter your new password in the boxes provided.

4. Click **Update Profile**.

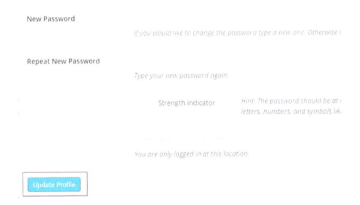

5. To Log Out of your site, move the cursor to the upper right corner of your screen and let the cursor hover over the word **Howdy** on the Dashboard.

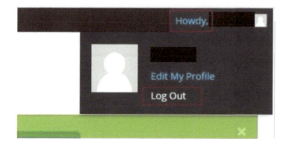

6. Click **Log Out**. By logging out you leave your website's control panel, i.e. the Dashboard.

You don't need to use all of the management features on the Dashboard, but you can learn more about them by visiting Wordpress.org and entering the search term in the search box.

Management Features on the Left Sidebar

On the Dashboard in the admin panel of your website, you will find a list of buttons that you can use to make changes to your website. You can use these buttons to create a post or page, change the appearance of your site, upload media, install plugins, add widgets to the sidebar of your site, manage comments, and change the settings of your site. Each of these tools will be explained. Let us start with changing the appearance of your website.

How to Change the Appearance of Your Website

When someone visits the home page of your WordPress site, they are looking at the "frontend" of your site, that is, the appearance of your site. You can change the way your site looks by downloading and installing a different WordPress theme.

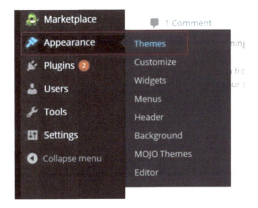

How to Change the Theme

1. Hover the cursor on **Appearance** on the sidebar and then click **Themes**.

2. To change the theme click on **Live Preview** on one of the pre-installed themes. If you like the way theme looks on your website then click **Save & Activate**.

3. If you don't like the theme then close it by clicking on the 'X' on the left side. You will be returned to the Themes page.

If you want to use a different theme then you can do a WordPress theme search in Google. There are many websites which offer free WordPress themes. Because Google has changed its algorithms and is now giving priority to mobile friendly websites, I highly recommend that you install a mobile friendly theme. These types of themes are called Responsive Themes. These are some of the websites I visit to find professional-looking responsive WordPress themes which you can download for free:

http://wordpress.org/themes/browse/popular

http://www.hongkiat.com/blog/free-responsive-wordpress-themes/

http://designscrazed.org/free-responsive-wordpress-themes/

http://premium.wpmudev.org/blog/30-free-responsive-and-stunning-wordpress-themes/

4. Select the theme you want and click **Preview**, or **Live Demo**.

5. If you like the way the theme looks then click **Download**. The theme will download to your computer hard drive as a Zip file. Most likely the Zip file will be saved in your Downloads folder.

6. Under Themes in your WordPress site, click **Add New** in order to upload your new theme.

7. Click on **Choose File** and select the Zip file which contains your new WordPress theme and click **Open**.

8. Then click **Install Now** so that the Zip file will be uploaded to your WordPress site.

9. Once the theme has been installed successfully, you can either click **Live Preview** to have an idea of what the theme would look like on your site or you can click **Activate** so that your new theme will be live.

Installing Theme from uploaded

Depending on the theme you chose, you can make changes to the title, header image, background colour, and much more!

How to Change the Settings of Your Site

You may see a lot of sub-categories under Settings, but I will only go through the General and Reading settings for now because these are important. It is optional if you want to make changes to the Writing, Discussion, Media and Permalinks settings.

General Settings

1. Hover the cursor over **Settings** on the sidebar.

2. Click **General**.

3. Change the title and tagline of your website.

4. Enter your email address. You can also change the time zone and date format.

5. Scroll to the bottom of the page and click **Save Changes**.

General Settings

Your site is currently displaying a 'Coming Soon' page. Once you are ready to lau

Site Title	My Job Hunting Tips
Tagline	Best Tips to Help You Find a Job
	In a few words, explain what this site is about.
WordPress Address (URL)	http://www.myjobhuntingtips.com
Site Address (URL)	http://www.myjobhuntingtips.com
	Enter the address here if you want your site ho
E-mail Address	you@example.com
	This address is used for admin purposes, like n

Reading Settings

This section allows you to make adjustments to the way the website looks on its front page. You can either allow all of your blog posts to show or just simply have a static page at the front of your website. A static web page is one that contains fixed content. It shows the same information to every visitor to your site.

The following instructions will show you how to change the reading settings of your website.

1. Hover the cursor over **Settings** and then click **Reading**. This is where you can change the display of your front page. You can either have your blog appear on the front page or on a static page.

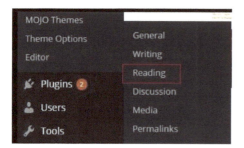

2. If you want a static page to be on the front page then you first need to create a page for your blog. Click on **Pages** on the sidebar. Refer to the instructions on *How to Create a Page* in the following chapter. You can use the word **Blog** as the title of your page.

3. Create a static page and use **Home** as the title.

4. Next to **Front Page Displays** select a **Static Page** and select **Home** for the Front Page and **Blog** for the Posts Page.

5. Scroll down to the bottom of the page and click **Save Changes**.

Reading Settings

Your site is currently displaying a "Coming Soon" page. Once you are ready to la

How to Create a Post

Posts have a title and body text where you can type your content. These posts appear in chronological order starting with the newest post at the top and the oldest post at the bottom. These posts make up what you call a blog and it can show up to 20 posts on your blog if you want it to.

1. Click on **Posts**, or **All Posts**, under the dashboard menu on the left sidebar.

2. Click **Add New**. (You can also click **All Posts**, which opens the **Posts** page. At the top click on **Add New**.) Either way, the edit page for posts will open with a blank section where you can create your first post.

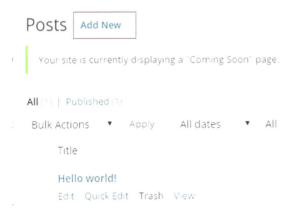

3. Type in your information. You can either click **Publish** so that your post will be published immediately on your site for the entire world to see, or you can click **Save Draft** if you are not ready to publish it yet and want to work on it later.

4. To view your post from the front end of your website click **View Post.**

How to Create a Page

Pages are similar to posts in that they have a title and body text, but they are different in that they are not a part of the chronological blog stream. In other words, pages in a WordPress website are static, meaning that they always display the same content. It never changes. Posts in a blog, however, are dynamic, in that they are constantly changing, usually on a daily or weekly basis.

There are two ways to create a page in WordPress:

Hover the cursor over **Pages** under the Dashboard menu on the left sidebar and click **Add New** to create a new page on your site.

The other way is to click on **Pages** or **All Pages** and then click **Add New** at the top of the page.

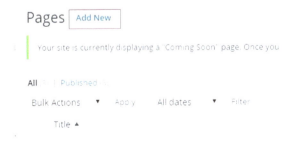

This is where you would create a new page for Contact, About Us, or Products page. These pages are known as static pages, in that they are not placed in chronological order like the blog posts.

Once you type in your information, click **Save Draft** if you want to save your work and then come back to it later.

Click on **Preview** to see what your page will look like on the front end of your website.

When you have completed your page, click on **Publish** so that the page will be published immediately.

After you have published your page, the Publish button will change to **Update**. If you make any changes to your page after it has been published, click on the **Update** button to save changes.

Then click **View Page** to see how your page looks on the frontend of your website.

If you decide that you no longer need the page and want to delete it from your website permanently, then click **Move to Trash**.

Delete a Page

There are two ways you can delete a page that was created.

1. In the page you are editing, simply click on the words in red **Move to Trash.** This method was briefly explained above.

2. Click **Pages** on the left sidebar. Hover the cursor over the title of the page you want to delete and click **Trash.**

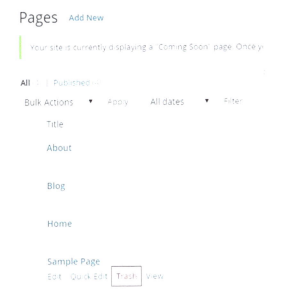

A notice will appear at the top of the page stating that the item has been moved to the Trash. You also have the option here to undo the deletion of the page.

Posts can also be deleted using the same method.

How to Upload Media

There are two ways to add media to your posts and pages simply by using the media button. One way is to click on the media button located in the post or page you are editing.

1. When editing a post, for example, click the **Add Media** button. A new window will open up.

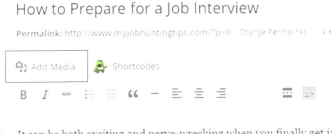

2. Ensure that the **Upload Files** tab is selected. If you have a picture saved on your hard drive, then click **Select Files**. You can also drag a file from your folder to add to the media library on your website.

3. Go to your folder where you have saved your photos or pictures and select the one you want to insert. You can then type in a title and alternate text for the picture.

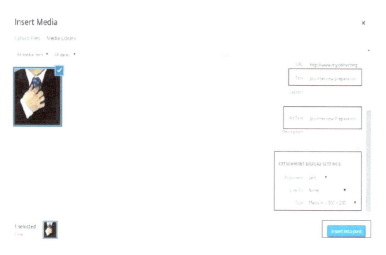

4. Enter the title of your image and the Alternate (Alt) text.

5. Under **Attachment Display Settings**, select the option to align the image to the left, right, or centre of the page.

6. Select whether you want the image to be linked to a particular website or the web page where you can see a larger size of the image, or you can select none so that it will not be linked to any web page.

7. Your image will then be uploaded into the media library in which you can then insert into your post. Click **Insert into post**.

8. If you don't like the image you chose click **Delete Permanently**, marked in red, located on the top right hand side, to get rid of the image. Then close the window.

9. Click **Publish** if you are publishing the page for the first time, or click **Update** if you are making changes to the page.

10. Click **View Post** to switch to the front end of your website and you will see the new post with your image included that you just published.

The other way to upload media is to add new images or other files to the Media Library.

One of the advantages of using WordPress is that you are not restricted to just uploading images alone. You can also upload PDF files, videos, music, Word documents, Excel spreadsheets, and PowerPoint presentations. These types of files can be uploaded to the Media Library.

1. Click on the **Media** button on the left sidebar or click **Library** under Media if you want to see what's in the Media Library. If you want to add new media then click **Add New**. In this case we want to add new media.

2. In the **Upload New Media** window you have the option to either select files from your computer, or drag and drop files into the **Media Library**.

3. Click **Select Files** and from your folder select the file you want to upload. Your file will upload instantly and you will see it below in the **Upload New Media** window. As an example, I uploaded an image file to the Media Library.

Upload New Media

Your site is currently displaying a "Coming Soon" page. Once you are ready to launch your site click here.

Select Files

You are using the multi-file uploader. Problems? Try the browser uploader instead.

Maximum upload file size: 50 MB.

4. To view the media files you uploaded click on **Library** under **Media**. The new media file that was uploaded is the first image shown on the left of the Library.

Media Library Add New

Your site is currently displaying a "Coming Soon" page. Once you are ready to

All media items ▼   All dates   ▼   Bulk Select

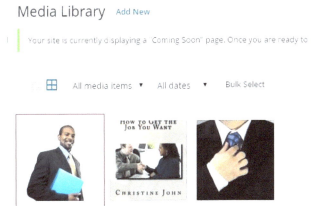

Delete Media

1. If you want to delete the media files you uploaded to the Media Library, then click on **Library** under **Media** on the left sidebar.

2. Click on the image that you want to delete. Click **Delete Permanently**.

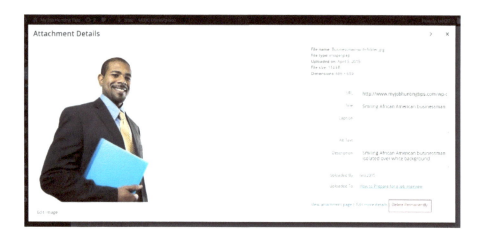

3. A pop up box will appear asking you to confirm whether you wanted to delete the file. Click **OK**.

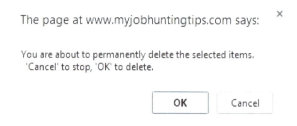

You cannot undo what you deleted in the Media Library.

How to Install Plugins

Plugins are WordPress tools that you can use to enhance certain functions of your site. There are plugins you can use to create forms, to block spam comments, to optimize your site, and so much more.

Install and Activate a Plugin

1. Click on **Plugins** under the dashboard menu and click **Add New**. The Install Plugins page will come up.

2. On the Install Plugins page type in a keyword and press Enter on the keyboard.

3. For example, let us search for the **Exclude Pages** plugin. This plugin allows you to choose which pages you don't want to appear on the navigational pages menu at the top of your website.

4. When you find the Exclude Pages plugin, click on **Details** to read more about the plugin and then click **Install Now** and the plugin will be immediately installed onto your site.

Sometimes the plugin you want to install may not be compatible with your current WordPress software. All plugins indicate how compatible they are with your current version of WordPress.

Always ensure that you install a plugin that is compatible with your software or else it may have a negative impact on the overall function of your website and it can also cause other plugins you installed not to work properly. An outdated plugin can also allow hackers to hack into your website.

You can see in the image above that the Exclude Pages plugin was updated 3 months ago and is compatible with the current version of WordPress which is version 4.1.1.

5. Click **Activate Plugin** to make the plugin active and then follow the instructions on how to configure the plugin if it is required.

Installing Plugin: Exclude Pages, Tags, Posts, L Apps) 1.0.9

Your site is currently displaying a "Coming Soon" page. Once you are ready to

Downloading install package from http://downloads.wordpress.org/plugin/e

Unpacking the package

Installing the plugin

Successfully installed the plugin Exclude Pages, Tags, Posts, Links & Categories

Activate Plugin | Return to Plugin Installer

The newly installed plugin will appear in the list on the Plugins page.

58

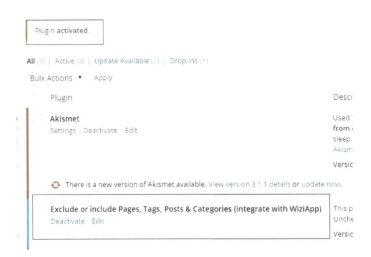

Instructions on how to use the plugin are usually included when it is installed in WordPress.

Delete a Plugin

1. Click **Installed Plugins** under the **Plugins** menu on the sidebar.

2. Find the plugin that you want to delete and first click **Deactivate** to stop the plugin from working on your website.

3. A message will appear at the top of the page stating that the selected plugin has been deactivated. Then click **Delete**.

4. You will be prompted to confirm that you want to delete the plugin and all its files. Click **Yes, delete these files**.

You will then be returned to the Plugins page and you will see a message at the top which states that the selected plugin has been deleted.

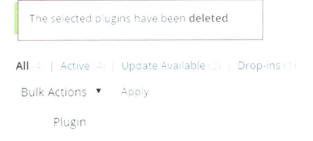

Other Useful Tools for Your WordPress Site

There are many other useful plugins that you can use to enhance the functionality of your WordPress website. Some are listed here, but you can find many more plugins at http://wordpress.org/plugins/browse/popular.

Akismet - one of the most popular spam blocker plugins for WordPress. You need to sign up for a free WordPress.com account to get an API key so that you can install and activate this plugin.

To get started, click on **Plugins** on the sidebar on the backend of your site and click **Activate** under the Akismet plugin.

A message will appear at the top of the page prompting you to activate your Akismet account. Click the blue button.

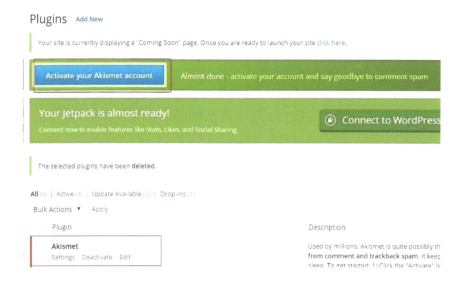

You will then be taken to the plugin's official site where you can get your API key. Click on the blue button and follow the instructions to get your Akismet API key. If you do not have a WordPress.com account then you will have to set up one in order to get access to the Akisment API key.

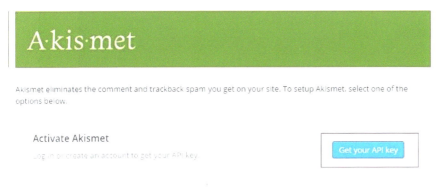

Once you have created your WordPress.com account, choose which package you want to use. You can either sign up for the Personal, Business, or Enterprise package. I usually select **Personal** and then click **Sign Up**.

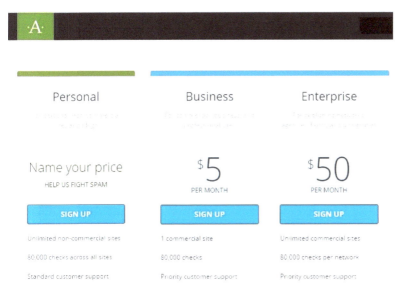

Next, select how much you want to pay to use Akismet to protect your website from spam and click **Continue**.

You will then be supplied with your own API Key with instructions on how to use it on your website.

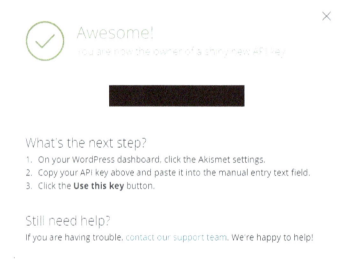

When you get the API key, copy the key, go back to your WordPress site and paste the API key in the field box next to the phrase **Manually enter an API key**. Click **Save Changes**.

You will receive a message that your Akismet plugin has been successfully activated. Below this message are options that you can select to further protect your website from spam. Select the option you require and then click **Save Changes**.

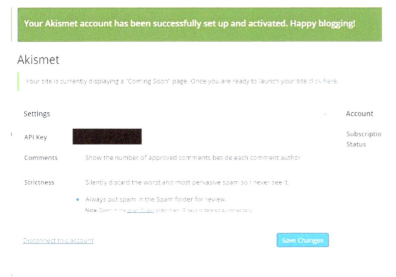

Now that you have activated the Akismet plugin your website will be protected from spam comments.

All in One SEO Pack – use this plugin to optimize your site for the search engines. Enter the title, description, and keywords to optimize your pages and posts.

Exclude Pages, Tags, Posts, Links and Categories – this plugin allows you to hide or exclude content from your desktop website or from your mobile app. If you don't want your content to appear to your website visitors then you can simply uncheck the checkbox which prevents users from seeing this content on your website.

Fast Secure Contact Form – this plugin allows you to insert a contact form on your Contact page. The form consists of Name, Email, and text area for the user to write a message. It also has a Submit button.

StatCounter – this is not a plugin, but it is a very useful tool that you can use to analyse the number of visitors to your website. It shows the number of daily, weekly, monthly, yearly, and quarterly visits to your site and where these visitors come from. Go to http://statcounter.com to get started.

Feedburner – if you want visitors to subscribe to your blog or newsletter, you can do it very easily with Feedburner. You can use this tool to distribute your content as feeds. It also provides you with the html code to place a subscription form on your website. You can place the form as a widget on your sidebar or anywhere on your pages or posts. To join feedburner you must have a Gmail account. Go to www.feedburner.com to get started. There is a lot you need to do to set up feedburner on your website so I suggest that you read the step by step guide to set up feedburner at http://www.wpbeginner.com/beginners-guide/step-by-step-guide-to-setup-feedburner-for-wordpress/.

Social Media Buttons – there are many social media plugins that you can install on your website to make it more interactive. You can have floating social media buttons or you can place them on the sidebar as a widget on your site. You can also place social media buttons anywhere on your posts or pages. Two social media plugins that you can install on your website are Social Media Feather and Floating Social Media Icon. These plugins can be found at Wordpress.org and you can access them from the Plugins page through your WordPress site.

Sitemap – This is another useful plugin that you can install on your site. The sitemap plugin helps search engines like Google, Bing, and Yahoo to better index your site. This tool is a must-have for every WordPress site. Just look for Google XML Sitemaps at Wordpress.org.

How to Manage Comments

Visitors to your site have the option of leaving a comment after reading your blog. You may receive positive comments, negative comments, or spam. The Comments menu under the dashboard allows you to manage comments that come into your site. You can easily delete the comments you don't want to appear below your blog and select those which you consider to be spam.

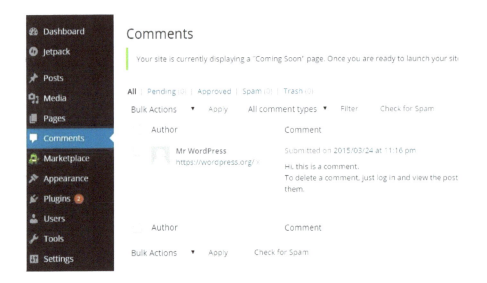

Because the website is new, the only comment displayed is a sample comment from WordPress.org.

Remove Comments from Pages

You can choose whether you want to display comments on your pages and posts.

If you do not want to display comments on your pages click on the **Pages** button on the sidebar.

Hover the cursor over one of the pages you want to change and click **Quick Edit**.

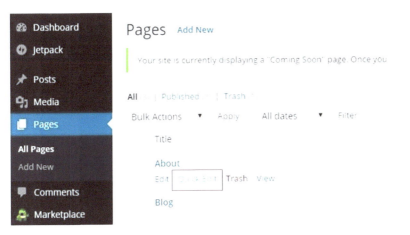

Uncheck the checkbox next to **Allow Comments**. Click **Update**.

Remove Comments from Posts

There may be certain posts that you have published to your blog that you don't want people to comment on. You can also remove comments from each of your posts.

1. Click on **Posts** on the sidebar.

2. Choose which post you want to remove comments from. Hover the cursor over the title and click **Quick Edit**.

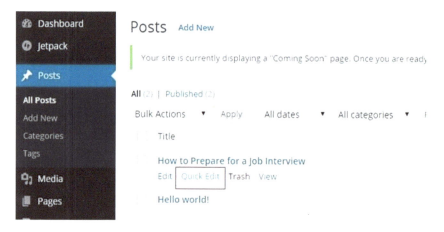

3. Uncheck the checkbox next to **Allow Comments** and click **Update**.

How to Use Widgets

Widgets are different, but very useful, tools that you can use to put content on your site without having to learn any complicated codes. Widgets normally appear on the sidebar of your WordPress site.

1. Once again hover the cursor over **Appearance** under the dashboard menu on the sidebar and then click **Widgets**. A page will open showing various widget buttons. Each widget has its own function and you can select the one you want to use according to your site's needs.

2. Then drag a widget from the widget area to the target sidebar and drop it where you want it to appear. For example, you can drag and drop a text widget into the sidebar area and then type something in the text area.

3. Drag the Text widget from the section under **Available Widgets** to the **Sidebar Widget Area**.

4. Enter a title in the Title box and type out a message. If you want each sentence to appear on a new line, then insert <br> between each sentence.

5. Click **Save** and then **Close**. The widget will appear on the sidebar of your site.

6. Click on **Visit Site** at the top left corner of the page in order to see the new widget added to your sidebar on the frontend of your website.

Sometimes having just plain text in a widget can make it look boring. You can spice up the appearance of your widget by including an image. In this case you will need to learn a little basic HTML in order for the image to appear in the widget.

1. If you have not done so already, upload an image that you want to include in your widget to be shown on your website. Go back to your Dashboard and hover the cursor over **Media** and click on **Add New**. Then you can upload or choose the image you want to use.

2. Once you have uploaded your image to the Media Library, click on **Edit**.

3. Copy the URL for the image, located on the right side of the page. First click inside the URL field and press **Ctrl +A** on the keyboard to select the whole URL. Then right click on the highlighted URL and click **Copy**.

4. Hover the cursor over Appearance in the sidebar and click on **Widgets**.

5. Click on the Text widget that you added to the sidebar and paste the URL at the top of the text box.

6. Now add some HTML codes to the Text widget to make the image appear and to make adjustments to the text.

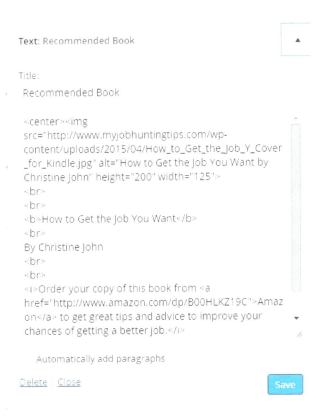

I know I said that you do not need to know any complicated HTML codes to design your website. Using HTML to design a widget is purely optional. However, it is good to learn a little HTML coding so that you can further develop your website and make it look the way you want it to without hiring some expensive web designer.

Do not be afraid of using HTML codes. It is not as complicated as it looks. Using simple HTML codes can make your website look more attractive and interesting. It can also grab the attention of your site visitors.

For example, you can use the following HTML code to insert an image into a widget:

```
<img src="image.jpg" alt="Image" height="150" width="150">
```

The <img> tag defines an image in an HTML page. Images are usually linked to HTML pages. It does not need a closing tag.

"Src" is where the image is coming from. It could be an image from your computer or it can be from the media library in WordPress. You can even get the URL for images from other websites.

"Alt" is the alternate text that you use to describe what the image is. If an image does not open in your web browser, you can still have an idea of what the image looks like by reading the alt text.

The width and height defines the dimensions of the image. You may have to do a little guess work and experiment with the dimensions. The width and height are usually measured in pixels. When placing an image in a widget on the sidebar, depending on the width of the sidebar, I recommend a maximum width of 200 pixels and a maximum height of 600 pixels.

As an example, the code for the image I placed in the widget is:

```
<img src="http://www.myjobhuntingtips.com/wp-content/uploads/2014/05/Get-a-Job-Book-Cover2.jpg" alt="How to Get the Job You Want by Christine John" height="200" width="125">
```

The source (src) of the image came from the WordPress media library in my website.

Use the following HTML code for a text link (a hyperlink) to link text to a particular web page:

<a href="URL" target="_blank">Link Text</a>

The HTML <a> tag defines a hyperlink. A hyperlink (or link) is a word, group of words, or image that you can click on to jump to another web page.

The href attribute specifies the destination of a link which will display like this: Visit Christine John Books.

Clicking on this hyperlink will send the user to Christine John Books' homepage.

The target attribute (target="_blank") specifies where to open the linked document.

The following example will open the linked document in a new browser window or a new tab:

<a href="http://www.christinejohnbooks.com" target="_blank">Visit Christine John Books</a>

The <center> tag places all images and text in the centre of the area where it is being positioned. Always ensure that you place </center> tag at the end of the image or text you wanted to align in the centre.

The <b> tag allows you to make text **bold**. Make sure that you place the closing </b> tag at the end of the text.

The <br> tag allows you to start text or to place an image on a new line. This does not need a closing tag.

The following example shows the HTML codes used in the text widget and how it appears on the frontend of the website in the sidebar:

<img src="http://www.myjobhuntingtips.com/wp-content/uploads/2014/05/Get-a-Job-Book-Cover2.jpg" alt="How to Get the Job You Want by Christine John" height="200" width="125"> How to Get the Job You Want By Christine John Order your copy of this book from <a href="http://www.amazon.co.uk/How-Get-Job-You-Want/dp/1490431756/ref=sr_1_1?ie=UTF8&qid=1401095046&sr=8-1&keywords=how+to+get+the+job+you+want+christine+john">Amazon</a> to get great tips and advice to improve your chances of getting a better job. 	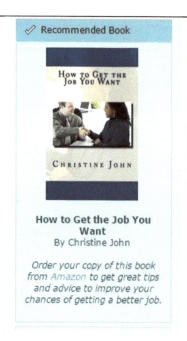

Delete a Widget

1. From the front end of the website hover the cursor over **My Job Hunting Tips** and click on **Widgets**. This will take you back to the Widgets page.

2. Click on the widget you want to delete that is located under the heading Sidebar. In this case, we want to delete the text widget that has the title 'Jobs Available'.

3. When the widget opens up, click **Delete**. This is not something that you can undo so be sure that the widget is something that you want to delete permanently.

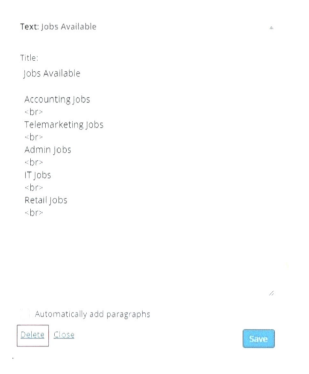

Remove a Widget

There may be times when you want to remove a widget from the sidebar but you don't want to delete it. You can do this by moving the widget to the **Inactive Widgets** area at the bottom of the Widgets page.

On the Widgets page select the widget you want to remove from the sidebar. Drag the widget from the **Sidebar Widgets** area to the **Inactive Widgets** area.

For example, if you wanted to remove the **Recent Comments** widget from the sidebar, simply click on the widget and drag it from the **Sidebar Widget** area to the **Inactive Widgets** area.

Inactive Widgets

Drag widgets here to remove them from the sidebar but keep their settings.

Recent Comments

Meta

Then click on **Visit Site** to ensure that the Recent Comments widget has been removed from the sidebar.

Optimize Your WordPress Site for the Search Engines

It is very important to optimize your WordPress site for the search engines because it helps you to improve your rankings on Google, gain more subscribers to your blog and it helps you to have a better website. Optimizing your site is a lot of work, but it is not difficult to do and when you are done, you will be pleased with the end result.

Search Engine Optimization simply means integrating the best searched for keywords into your post titles, pictures, descriptions, videos, and in your site's content. The WordPress tags are also very useful in optimizing your site.

Change Permalinks

The first thing you need to do to optimize your website is to change the permalink structure. Permalinks are web URLs that WordPress uses to create links to your categories and posts.

Go to **Settings** and click **Permalinks**.

The default permalink is set to *http://www.myjobhuntingtips.com/?p=123*.

Permalink Settings

Your site is currently displaying a "Coming Soon" page. Once you are ready to launch your site click here.

By default WordPress uses web URLs which have question marks and lots of numbers in them; however, WordPress offers you the ability to c permalinks and archives. This can improve the aesthetics, usability, and forward-compatibility of your links. A number of tags are available, an

Common Settings

- Default   http://www.myjobhuntingtips.com/?p=123

  Day and name   http://www.myjobhuntingtips.com/2015/04/01/sample-post/

  Month and name   http://www.myjobhuntingtips.com/2015/04/sample-post/

  Numeric   http://www.myjobhuntingtips.com/archives/123

  Post name   http://www.myjobhuntingtips.com/sample-post/

  Custom Structure   http://www.myjobhuntingtips.com

It is recommended that you use either the post name permalink or the category/post name permalink.

To change the permalink settings for the first option, simply click on Post name. Your permalink structure will then be set to
http://www.myjobhuntingtips.com/sample-post.

To include categories in your permalinks click Custom Structure and enter the value */%category%/%postname%/*. Your permalink structure will then change to *http://www.myjobhuntingtips.com/%category%/%postname%/*.

When you are finished click the button **Save Changes**. The permalink structure will be updated and WordPress will redirect the links to your posts.

Optimize the Titles of Your Posts for SEO

It is important that you optimize the title and content of your website so that your site will rank high in search results. You need to make it so that your website can be found on the first page of search results of search engines like Google, Yahoo, and Bing.

Optimizing your titles simply means finding the right keywords that your target audience searches for on a monthly basis. You can find out what people search for by using the Google Keyword Planner. Look for keywords that have high global monthly searches but low competition.

For example, I wanted to write a post about job interviews. I searched for the keyword 'job interviews' in the Google Keyword Planner. What I found was that the keyword 'job interview questions' had over 300,000 global monthly searches and low competition. This is the keyword I would use within the title of my blog post. Therefore my post title would be *"Top Ten Job Interview Questions and How to Answer Them"*.

Optimize the Descriptions of Your Posts/Pages

It is also important to optimize the description of your website content so as to grab the attention of the search engines. The description of your content is usually found beneath the URL on the search results pages. The description should contain the same keywords you used in your title at least once. Your description should also contain persuasive text that entices the reader to click on the URL so that they can read more about what you are offering or what your post or page is about.

Optimize Your Images

When we are writing posts or creating pages and we insert images we often forget or neglect to optimize our images so that they can be indexed by different image search engines. Optimizing your images is very easy to do. You just need to optimize the title and the Alt tag of your images and this simple task can actually help you to gain more traffic to your website. It also helps users who may have older browsers to make sense of images that may be hidden to them.

To optimize your images, click on **Media** which will take you to the Media Library. Click **Edit** under the title of one of the images and change the title of the image using your best searched for keywords. Then scroll down until you see the description and Alternative Text below the image. Again type in your best keywords for the alternative text and the description. When you are finished click **Update**.

Optimize Your Tags

After you have written your post and inserted your image, in addition to optimizing the title and images, you can also optimize the post tags. All you have to do is include your best keywords that you used for the title, images, and description within your post's tags.

Tags

Add

Separate tags with commas

Choose from the most used tags

.

Click on **Pages** on the sidebar. Click **Edit** under the title of the post you want to make changes to. On the right sidebar of the Edit Post page you will find the heading Tags. Type in a keyword that is relevant to the post and click **Add**. Once you are finished click **Update**. It's that simple.

Now that you have done basic optimization of your website, you can now launch your site and submit it to the major search engines such as Google, Yahoo, and Bing. Please keep in mind that you need to have an email account with each of these sites in order to submit your website.

Go to your Dashboard on the backend of your website and click **'click here'** to launch your site.

Dashboard

Your site is currently displaying a "Coming Soon" page. Once you are ready to launch your site click here.

Then go to the following sites to submit your website for free:

Google http://www.google.com/submityourcontent/website-owner/

Yahoo http://search.yahoo.com/info/submit.html

Bing http://www.bing.com/toolbox/submit-site-url

Conclusion

Thanks to the explosion of the internet and the rapid development of information technology now is the best time to get your message out to the masses with your very own website. WordPress has made it very easy for anyone to set up a website or blog without any technical knowledge.

You can use the WordPress platform to do just about anything you can imagine from creating a photo blog to building an e-commerce store. WordPress provides thousands of different tools to enhance the functionality of your website.

This book is just a basic guide to creating your own WordPress website and I hope that you have found the information in this book useful. There is still so much more that you can discover about WordPress that can further develop your web designing skills.

A website never stays the same and you always have to make changes to it in order to fit in with the changes in your business and in your market. By using the tools mentioned in this book and doing your own research online for other WordPress themes and plugins, you can be sure that your website will continue to evolve to the point where you have developed it according to what your target audience wants and where you have finally achieved the objectives you had in mind when you purchased this book.

About the Author

Christine John was born in Bermuda and moved to the Commonwealth of Dominica when she was 14 years old. She studied at the University of the West Indies where she acquired a Bachelor's Degree in Management Studies. Presently Christine lives in the United Kingdom where she helps aspiring entrepreneurs to start and grow their businesses on the internet.

Christine is an experienced author and web designer. She enjoys writing non-fiction books on various business topics, short stories, and poetry. She also enjoys designing websites and is interested in small business and entrepreneurship, employment and careers, personal development, e-commerce, internet marketing, affiliate marketing and web designing.

Other Books Written by Christine John

Visit Amazon now to grab your copy of these other books. All books are available in print and Kindle formats.

How to Start and Run an Online Business

This is an easy step-by-step internet business guide that shows you how to create an online business of your own. This book will help you to come up with a great idea, decide on a product to sell, create a website or blog, build an ecommerce store, promote your site online for free, make money from your website/blog, and lots more! Read this step-by-step online business book to help you find out everything you need to know about starting an online business.

Amazon US: http://www.amazon.com/dp/B00877LA52

Amazon UK: http://www.amazon.co.uk/dp/B00877LA52

Short Stories for Teenagers

This book consists of six short stories about six different teenagers:

Pamela - Will she survive her date with a stranger?

Rachel - She won't let anything stop her from going to the prom, not even a baby.

Ryan - He finally got a date with one of the most popular girls in school, but will she give him what he's expecting to get from her?

Andrea - People keep talking about her and Jerry which is making her feel very uncomfortable. Should she sacrifice her friendship to end the gossip?

Judy - Bob bosses her around and treats her like dirt. Should she stay with him or find someone new?

Whitney - Jerome has been taking her for granted and she's sick of it. She found someone else who treats her better, but will it last?

Find out what happens to these six teenagers in these amazing short stories.

Amazon US: http://www.amazon.com/dp/B008BXBMG4

Amazon UK: http://www.amazon.co.uk/dp/B008BXBMG4

The Runaway Bride

This is a story about a woman named Serena who married the man of her dreams at a very young age. Feeling intimidated and threatened by her mother-in-law, Serena runs away to fulfil her dream of going to university to study art. But her plans are soon interrupted by a devastatingly handsome and charming stranger. Now Serena is feeling very confused about what she really wants.

Should she go back to her overprotective husband and endure the icy stares and cold, cruel insults of her horrible mother-in-law, or should she spend the rest of her days living a wild and exciting life with the very sexy Armando?

Amazon US: http://www.amazon.com/dp/B00CR0YPZW

Amazon UK: http://www.amazon.co.uk/dp/B00CR0YPZW

How to Get the Job You Want

This is a practical guide which provides you with the tools you need to find a job that you enjoy doing. The job market is very competitive and you need to have the right tools to stay one step ahead of all the other candidates in order to land a great job. This book is the solution to your job hunting needs. This comprehensive guide gives you great advice to assist you with your job search and is suitable for those who want to change their careers and for those who just graduated from high school or college. From writing CVs and cover letters to preparing for job interviews, this book contains everything you need to help you to find the job you want.

Amazon US: http://www.amazon.com/dp/B00HLKZ19C

Amazon UK: http://www.amazon.co.uk/dp/B00HLKZ19C

Last Chance

You only have one life and one chance to make things right.

Barry Briggs had been divorced for over a year and all he could think about was getting back together with his ex-wife, Margie. But Sheila, his current girlfriend, stood in his way of reconciling with his ex-wife.

Drowning in debt and feeling tired of his current relationship, Barry sets himself on a mission to accomplish three things: to break up with Sheila, become financially free, and rekindle his marriage.

But then a fatal heart attack, Sheila's pregnancy, and a dangerous man from Sheila's past send Barry's life spiralling out of control. Will Barry have time to put his life in order and get back together with Margie before it is too late?

Amazon US: http://www.amazon.com/dp/B00P0A08ZM

Amazon UK: http://www.amazon.co.uk/dp/B00P0A08ZM

Poems About Life

Poems About Life – A collection of poetry by the author Christine John.

Let yourself be swept away by this beautiful book of poetry. This book is divided into sections and talks about love, friendship, heartbreak, family, loneliness, disappointments and inspiration.

Life has its ups and downs, good times and bad times. The author of this book writes about different aspects of life such as a first kiss, moments of weakness, and the choices we face in life. She also talks about having faith in God and being able to look to heaven for guidance and inspiration. All it takes is to write a poem to give an individual the ability to express one's feelings about life.

Amazon US: http://www.amazon.com/dp/B00TOMK41A

Amazon UK: http://www.amazon.co.uk/dp/B00TOMK41A

www.ingramcontent.com/pod-product-compliance
Lightning Source LLC
LaVergne TN
LVHW012315070326
832902LV00001BA/12